The Really Easy Way To Play The Drums

by Steve Laffy

This book is dedicated to all drummers past, present and future.

I would like to give special thanks to my good friend Poli Palmer for his kindness and help, and for writing the music for *Show Time*. Thanks to Simon Laffy, Dan Patey, Sam Kelly and Ross Elder for their inspiration and encouragement. I am most grateful to Jason Flinter and to Graham White for front cover design, layout and video shots.

First published by Steve Laffy in 2003
ISBN 978-0-9544928-2-3
Kindle edition August 2012
Fifth edition revised January 2019

Available from www.learn-drums.co.uk

DVD 1 – The Really Easy Way to Play the Drums DVD
EAN No. 5 060211 970009

Book/CD2 – The Easy Way to Advance Your Drumming
ISBN 978-0-9544928-1-6

The sixteen accompanying video lessons are similar to the book text examples with new and different ideas, variations and additions in the same style.

QR Scan Audio Folder Here

QR Scan Video Folder Here

Contents

Welcome to the world of drumming

Congratulations for deciding to play the drums. Many people wish they could play this wonderful instrument, but few take the first step. You have. Well done!

Learning to play well will need time to develop your skills, and this will take persistence, patience and practice. It is worth it and you will get a lot of enjoyment for your efforts.

Let me tell you how I learned to play the drums. As a child there was no room in our house for a drum kit and no money for lessons, so I started by tapping out some beats on tins with pencils. I was a late starter, getting my first drum kit at 18 years of age. I played around on the kit for a few years learning bits and pieces, until the age of 21 years old when I decided (with the encouragement of others) that I would take it seriously and make it my profession. I soon realised I had a lot of hard work to do to reach a standard that would be required to be a professional musician. I started on a committed 3year study practising about 5 hours every day. I tried to learn as much as possible about all styles of music. I taught myself to read drum music notation, discovered the drum rudiments and listened to lots of great drummers. The study continues still today, some 35 years later. I have tried my very best to share this experience with you in this book.

You will find your own goals for learning the drums and decide how much time you are happy to dedicate to developing your skills, and I promise you will learn a lot about your self in the process.

Getting started is the hardest part of anything that is a challenge. I hope that this book and CD will help you on the way.

Drums have been around for thousands of years so you are joining a tradition with a long history. Now it's your tune to contribute to that history. You CAN do it!

10 Steps Skills Accomplished	
Step 1 Pages 8 - 12 Three-way independence using 1/8ths and 1/16ths around the kit with hands and bass drum. Recognition of music notation, various stickings, lengths of bars etc.	
Step 2 Pages 13 - 17 Playing a one bar beat with 1/4 and 1/8th notes with both hands and bass drum. Playing one bar of a rhythm and one bar of a fill, using 1/8th and 1/16th notes and reading notes of all of the drums including snare and tom toms.	
Step 3 Pages 18 - 19 Learning about all of the signs that we use to make our drumming sound more dynamic. Playing four bar phrases. Introduction to Funk Drumming and learning 1/8th note variations with the bass drum.	
Step 4 Pages 20 - 23 Drum phrases using parts of 1/16th notes. Introduction to the Rumba rhythm. More four bar phrases using the funky bass drum beats.	
Step 5 Pages 24 - 26 Playing with two hands together for fills, and 1/16th notes variations to make your own really interesting drum parts. Splitting 1/16th notes between drums, and opening hi hats. Learning to play another Latin rhythm.	
Step 6 Pages 27 and 28 Learning a new time signature, and how to in 3:4 time. Playing a 3:4 rock beat and fills. Discover more snare drum variations and playing a 4s snare Tamla Motown beat.	
Step 7 Pages 29 - 30 More beats using four-way independence and really developing the Rumba rhythm and increasing your understanding of different styles of music. Play Rock and Latin styles your second one page piece, and seeing how two different styles can work together.	
Step 8 Pages 31 - 32 Learn a whole new feel and style of playing, using Triplets. Master two new rhythms, the 12/8 triplet rhythm for use with slow songs, and the shuffle beat for up-tempo bouncy tunes. Introducing the jazz swing and half time shuffle too.	
Step 9 Page 33 Really getting in to Funk grooves and starting to use 1/16th notes on the high hat. Add to this the funky 1/8th note patterns on the bass drum (see page 19), and you are by now starting to really develop a solid style of playing..	
Step 10 Pages 34 - 35 The final challenge, playing and developing everything you have learned throughout the book.	

Warming up and good posture

It is important for preventing injury to always warm up your body - both on and off the kit, before playing the drums.
Before you sit at the kit stand tall, legs slightly apart, arms by your sides and roll your shoulders in big circles 5-6 times one way then the other. Now put your thumbs on your shoulders and make big circles with your elbows 5-6 times one way then the other. Now with your arms fully stretched, make circles as above.
Try and stay loose and relaxed at all times while playing the drums.
See www.learn-drums.co.uk for more warm up tips.

Picture 1
Sit up straight at the drum kit. Don't slouch over. Sit at a distance where you can reach everything comfortably.

Picture 2
Hold your sticks correctly. Hold firmly with your thumb and forefinger, letting the stick sit comfortably in the middle joint of your fingers. Hold the sticks raised away from the drums so you can come down with a good solid stroke.

The correct grip

Hold the sticks correctly and you will make a good sound from the drums, and be able to play without getting tired.

Picture 3
Hold the sticks so that you make a reverse V shape over the snare drum. Try and keep your knuckles upwards, not your thumbs. Keep your arms away from your sides with a little space between your arms and your body.

Picture 4
When playing the snare drum and hi hat, have the sticks crossing each other not the hands.
This example is for right handed players.
Stay relaxed and comfortable when you play, and if anything begins to ache, get off the drums and do the exercises described earlier.

The basics

Below is the stave. It is the space that drum notes are written on.
At the end of this stave are bar lines. They divide the stave into bars.

Each drum and cymbal is marked on separate lines as follows.

These are the most commonly used ones.

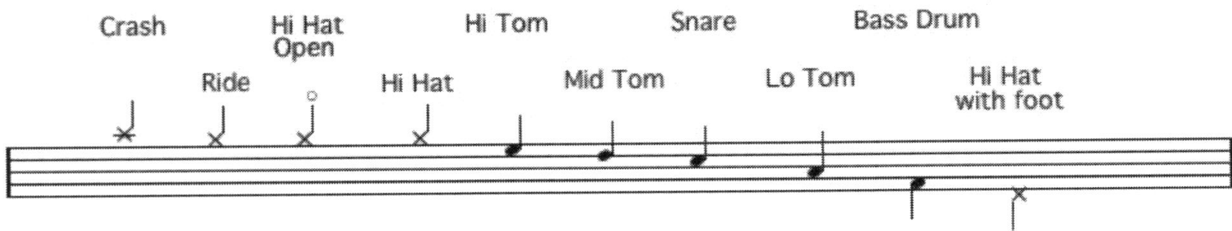

There are some variations to the above and will be shown in other books you may study.

Drum rhythms and patterns can be played with various hand combinations.
These are called stickings. Try the following stickings on your snare drum or practise pad.

(Left handed players can start with the left hand.)

Play all of the above starting slow and observe the hand and stick positions on Pages 8-9.
Gradually increase the speed, keeping it smooth and even.
Then gradually decrease the speed, back to slow and keeping it smooth and even.
Repeat the above exercise until you can play these stickings to a good speed.

The next page will show you how we divide a bar with various notes to make a rhythm.

Video 1

Easy Drum Notes

All you need to learn to get started with drumming are 3 easy notes 1/4s, 1/8s, and 1/16s.

If you break a bar of chocolate into 4 even pieces you will have quarters.
A bar of music divided into 4 pieces or sections are made with 1/4 notes.
Play them one beat with each hand (singles R L R L etc.) and count them out LOUD!

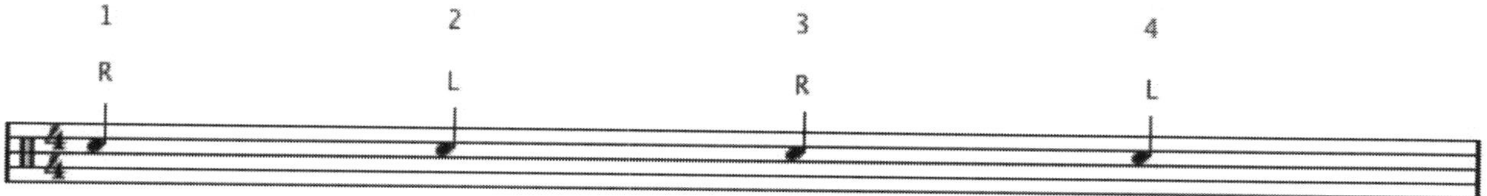

The two numbers at the beginning of the bar are called the time signature. This time signature tells you that this bar has four beats, and that they are 1/4 notes.

If you divide each 1/4 note into two you will then have1/8th notes. 1/8th notes in pairs have a single line on top joining them together.

Count this bar of 1/8 notes out loud, and play as singles (R L R L etc.)

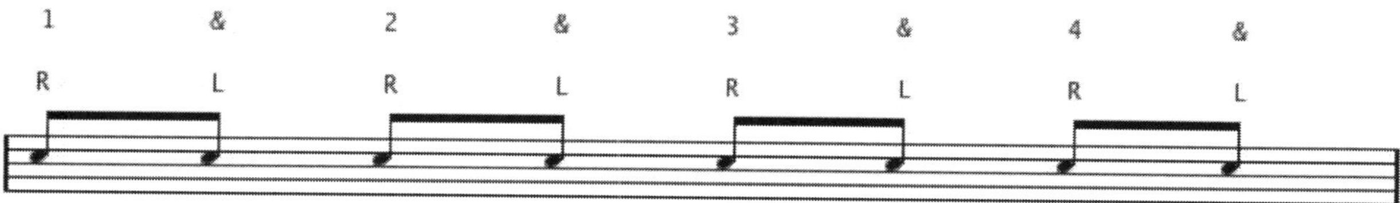

If you divide each 1/4 note into four you will then have 1/16th notes. 1/16th notes have a double line on top joining them together.

Count this bar of 1/16th notes out loud and play as singles.

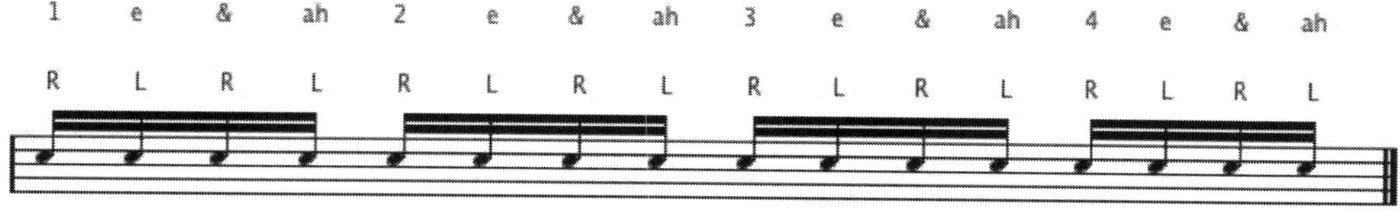

Adding the bass drum

So far we have just played with the hands. Now we can add the bass drum with your foot. Remember the bass drum is shown on the bottom line. The hands play on the snare drum.

Play these bars of 1/4s, 1/8s and 1/16s as singles and count out loud.
Once you can play them all smoothly try going for one bar into the next

Notice that the bass drum stays the same and the hands change to fit in the extra beats.

These two bars have 8s and 16s put together. Play as singles and count out LOUD!

Video 2

Around the kit

Play the bar of 8s below with single, double and paradiddle stickings.
Repeat each sticking individually, then go from one into the other.
Dedicate yourself to practising and you will become great at playing the drums!

Ex.1

Now practise 8s and 16s around the kit with all of the above stickings.

Ex.2

Now try the same two bars alternating bass drum and hi hat with the feet.

Ex.3

The doubles and paradiddles are more challenging, so continue with the rest of the book and come back to work more on these.

Video 3

Your first drum piece

Try and make the 1 bar fills more interesting by moving from the snare to the other drums in the kit. Notice when the notes move up and down to tell you to change to other drums.
To keep it simple we will just use the high and low toms at the moment.
Feel free to add the middle tom if you wish. Experiment and make up your own fills.

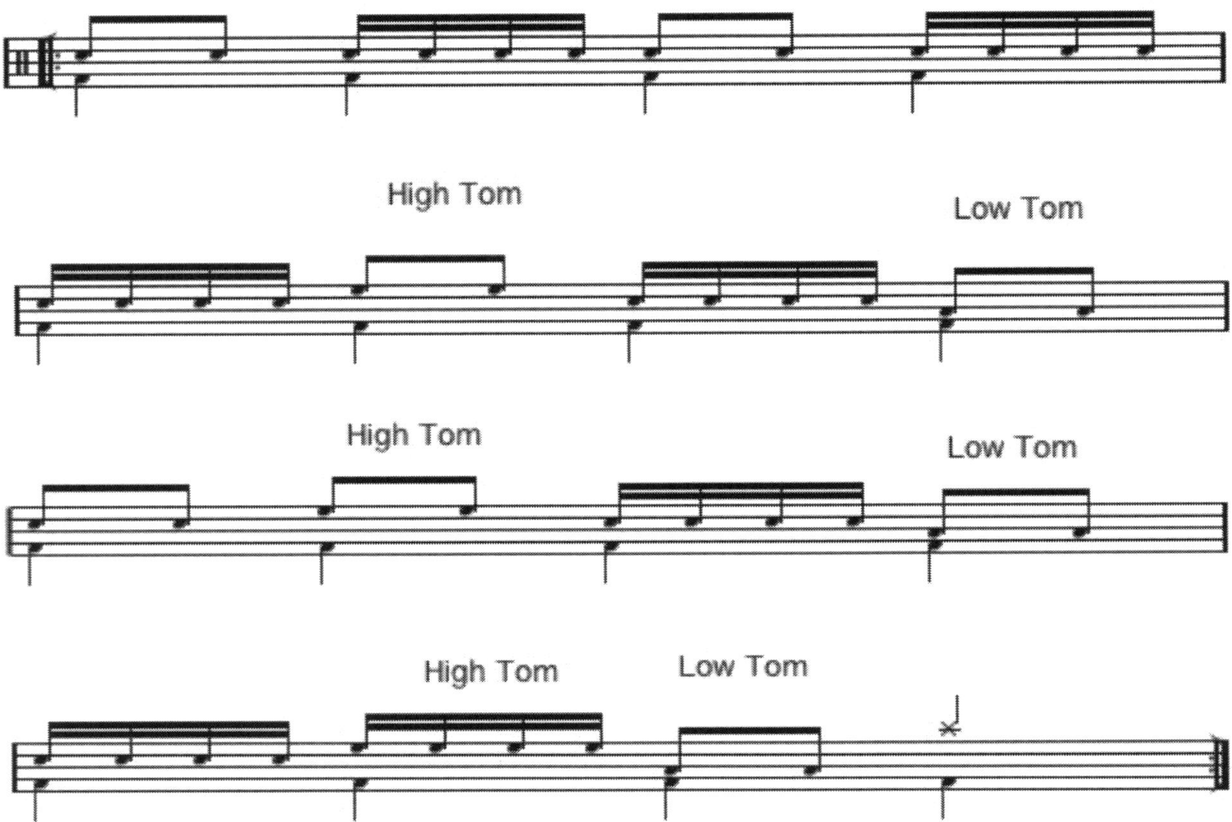

- Now try the same four bars alternating bass drum and hi hat with the feet.
- Make up your own four bar piece using the middle tom as well.
- Try and play the piece at a faster speed keeping it smooth and even.

Video 4

The first drum kit rhythm

(Using 1/4 notes)

Playing in co-ordination with your hands and feet together is one of the major aspects of playing the drum kit.
Here we will now play a rhythm on the kit using both hands and one foot using the bass drum the snare drum and the hi hat at the same time.
The hi hat plays four steady beats with one hand and the bass drum joins on the first beat.

Ex.1

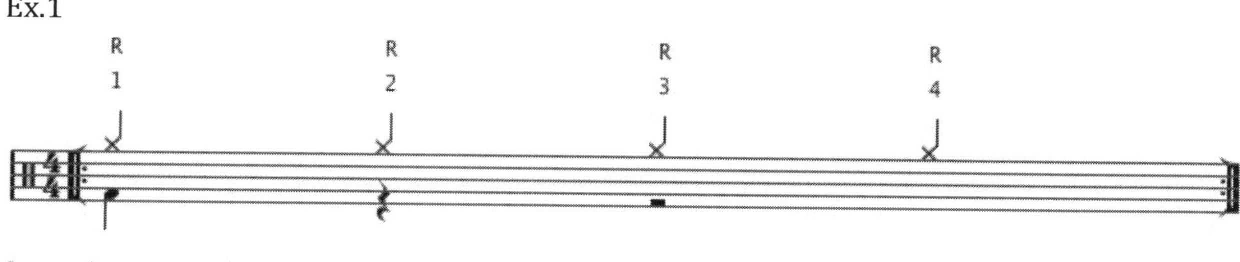

If we play some beats in a bar and not others we need to put a rest sign to account for the space not played.
The sign under the second beat is a 1/4 note rest, and the sign under the third beat is a 1/2 note rest.
So the bass drum part of this bar has:
One 1/4 note on beat one
One 1/4 note rest on beat two
One 1/2 note rest on beat three
1/4 + 1/4 + 1/2 = a whole bar of four 1/4 notes.

Now the hi hat plays four steady beats and the snare drum joins in on the third beat.

Ex. 2

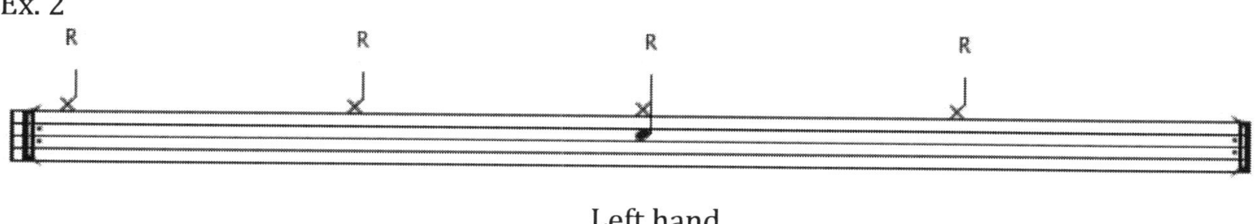

Left hand

As the snare note is joined with the hi hat on the third beat no rests are necessary.

The bass drum joins the hi hat on the first beat and the snare joins on the third beat.

Ex. 3

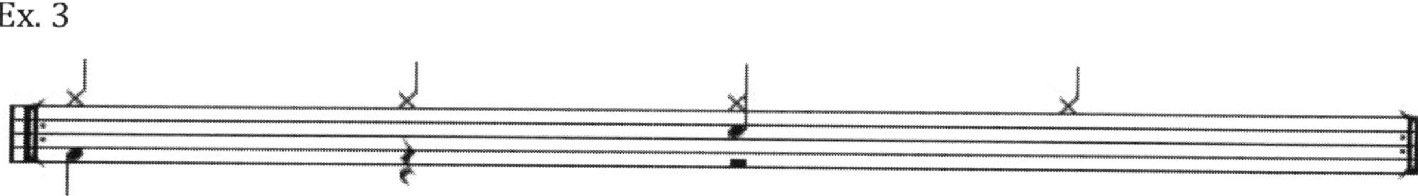

The 8s rock rhythm

(Using 1/8 notes)

This is the same use of hands and feet as the last page and now we are using 1/8th notes. The top line is played with your right hand (left hand if you are left handed) playing a steady and continuous bar of 1/8th notes on the high hat, with the bass drum joining in on beats one and three, and the snare drum joining in on beats two and four.
Counting out loud is very important and will help a lot in you understanding exactly where you are in each bar.

The hi hat plays eight steady beats and the bass drum joins in on the first and third.
Ex.1 Count

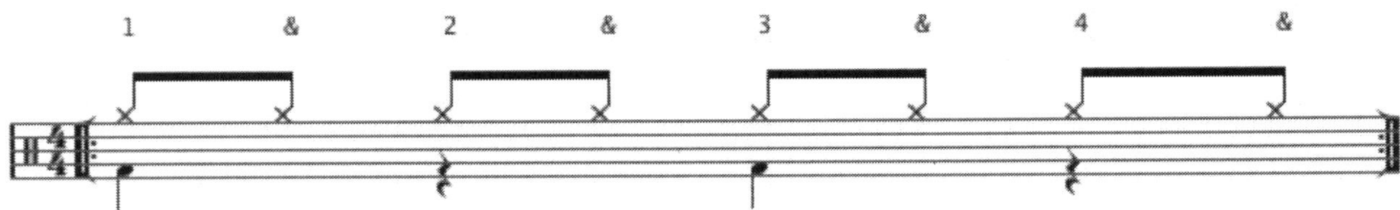

Now the snare joins the high hat on beats two and four.
Ex.2

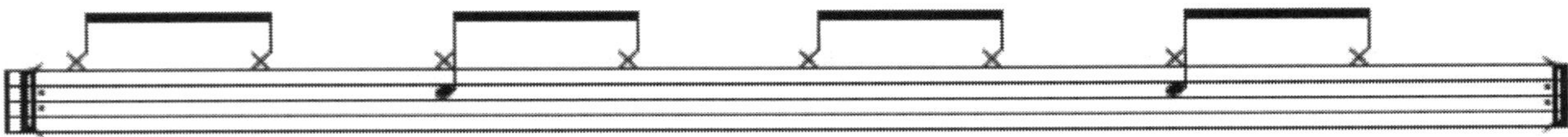

Here we play them all together.
Ex.3

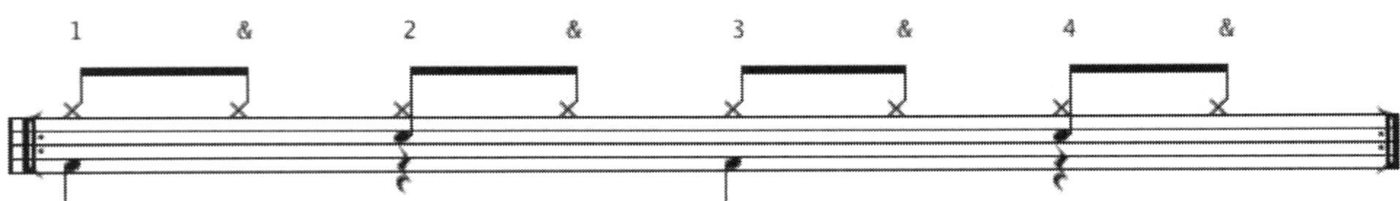

You could try moving your right hand to the cymbal and add the high hat with your foot.
Ex.4

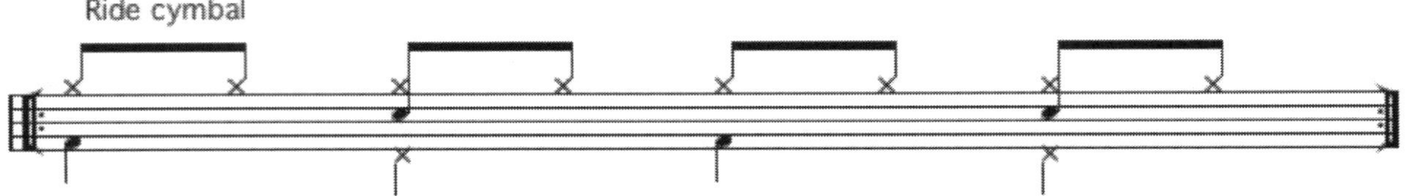

Video 5

The rhythm and the fill

Let's now play one bar of rhythm followed by a one bar fill of 8s.
Count throughout.

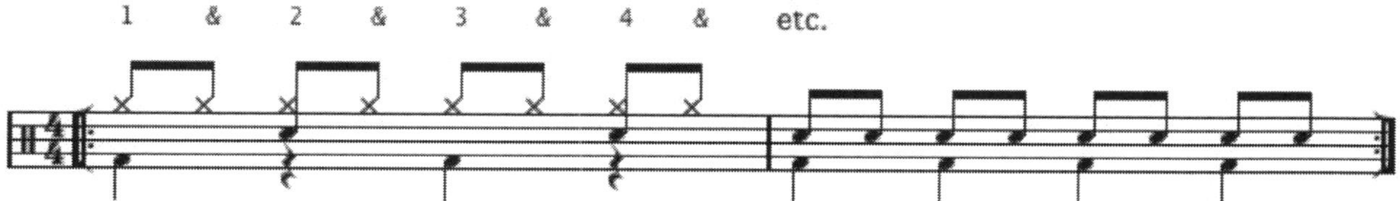

Repeat the same two bars above and play the bar of 8s fill between the snare and hi tom. Play the same between the snare and middle tom, then snare and lo tom. Practise until you get fluent and smooth, playing around all the drums.

You can start a fill on any drum, and don't have to move to a different drum each beat.

Like this...

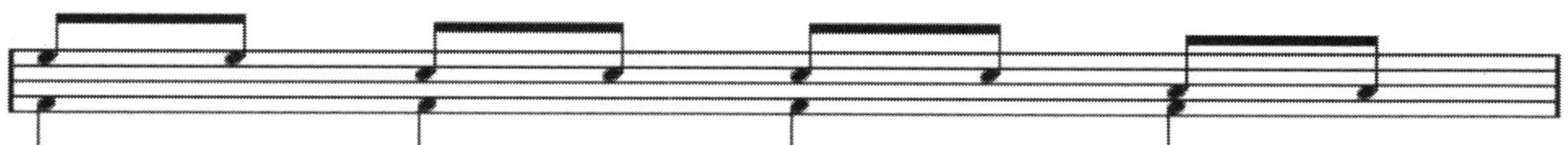

Try switching the hi hat hand to the ride cymbal, and add the hi hat played with the foot on beats two and four... and count loud throughout.

Fill It Up

Here's a whole piece using one bar of rhythm and one bar of fill. Count throughout.
Play right hand on ride cymbal or hi hat.
Hear how the sound changes when you open the high hat with the foot while you are playing it with the stick.
Play the crash cymbal on the very first beat of the bar, and hi hat or ride on the rest.
This sign is called an accent and it means you play this note louder than the other notes.

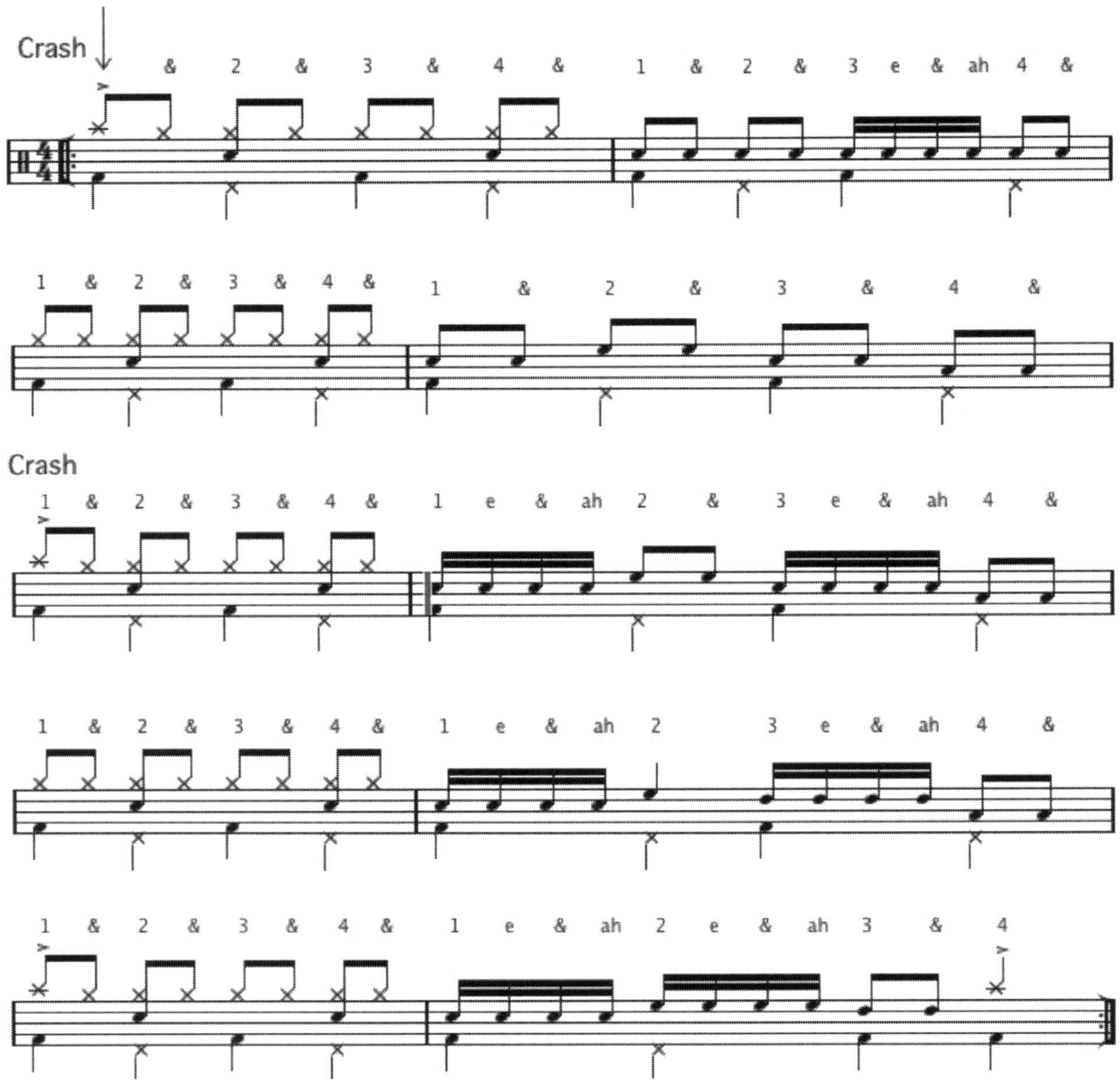

Video 6

Switch It Over

When you are playing tunes the tight controlled sound of the closed high hats work well in some sections (verses etc.) and the open sound of the ride cymbal in other places like choruses and solos.
It's good to get used to switching from high hat to cymbal with your leading hand. Usually a drum part will write when the high hat or the ride cymbal is required like in the piece below.

Video 7

Some more signs

Here are some more signs that give you direction in what to play. They also give the music more expression and make it sound better. Observe and play them all.
This sign tells you the speed (tempo) of this piece. 120 quarter notes in a minute.

♩= 120 Practise it slower at first and build up to 120 beats per minute (bpm)

mf This sign means play medium loud, until another sign tells you to change.

High Hat

This sign means repeat the last bar.

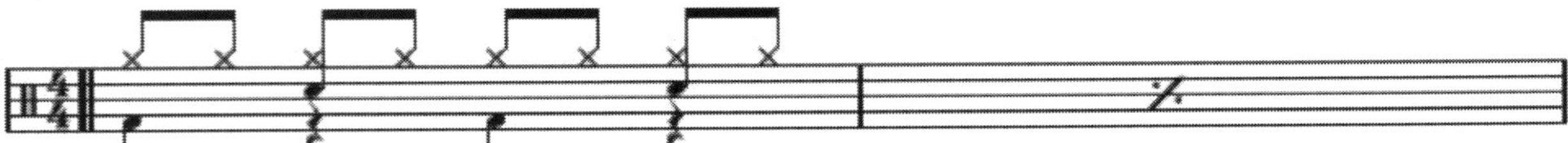

This is a diminuendo. Get gradually quieter.

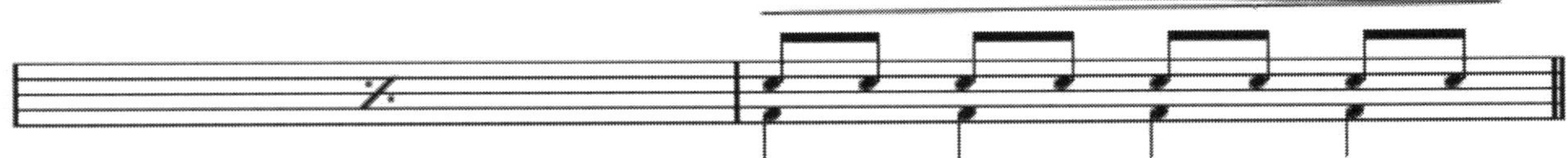

This sign means play quietly, until another sign tells you to change.

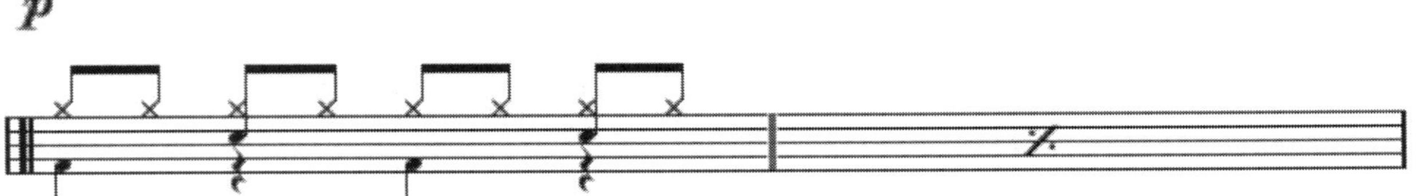

This is a crescendo. Get gradually louder.

This sign means play loud.

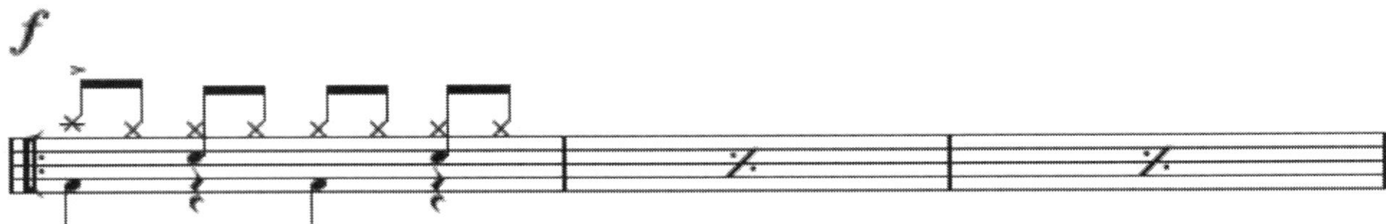

Bar 1 is played the first time through, then on the repeat play only the second time bar (2.)

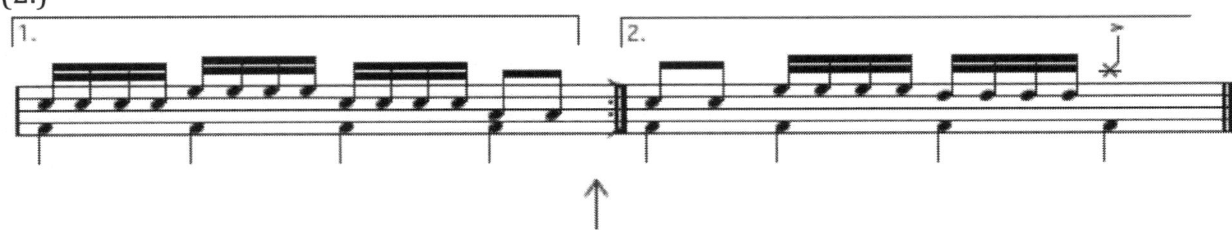

At this sign you go back to where you see the same sign before (the line above).

Video 8

Funky bass drum beats

Let's develop the bass drum patterns by adding various 1/8 note variations. The bass drum always falls with the hand playing 1/8 notes on the high hat.
Counting is essential to get the bass drum playing on the correct beat.

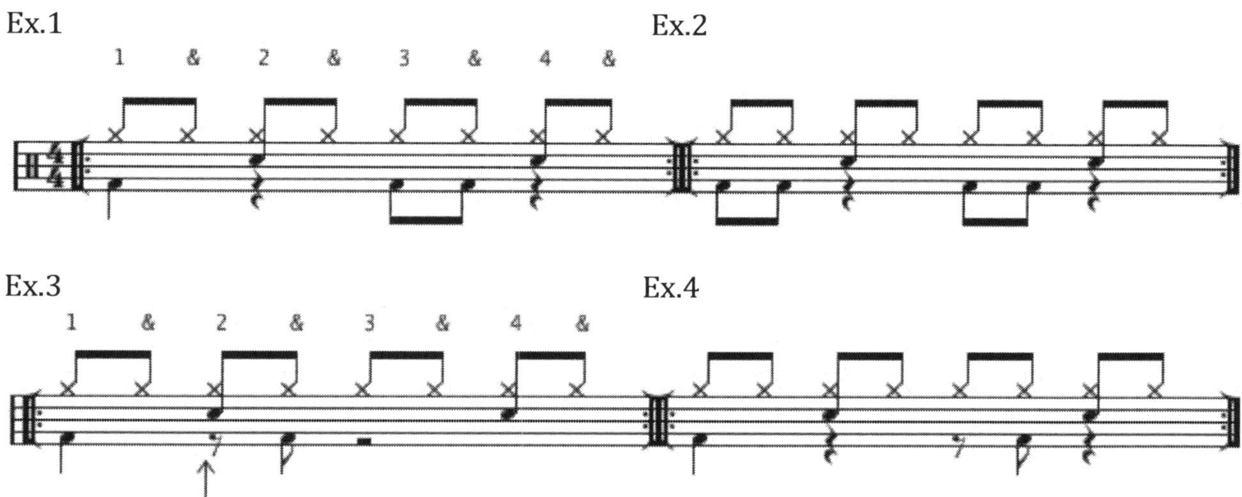

This sign here is an 1/8 note rest. 1/8 notes don't always have to be played as a pair, and when they are played separately notice they have a different tail. When we leave out the first 1/8 note we need to add an 1/8 note rest. Counting out loud really helps to understand this.

- Play these with the right hand on the hi hat and the ride.
- Add the hi hat with the foot on beats two and four on all of theses examples.
- Play these rhythms as two and four bar sequences and add your own fills.
- Also practise this page 1/8 and 1/16 notes with the right hand.

Video 9

Part groups of 16th notes

1/16 notes don't always have to be played as groups of four. They can be split into smaller groupings to make even more interesting rhythms.
In this grouping instead of playing all four notes we leave out the last one (the ah.) The sticking (which hands we play with) is important now as it usually works best to start each group of notes with your leading hand.

Notice the gap in the group of 1/16s here. Imagine the last note is left out.

Ex.1

Note the sticking.
Count...

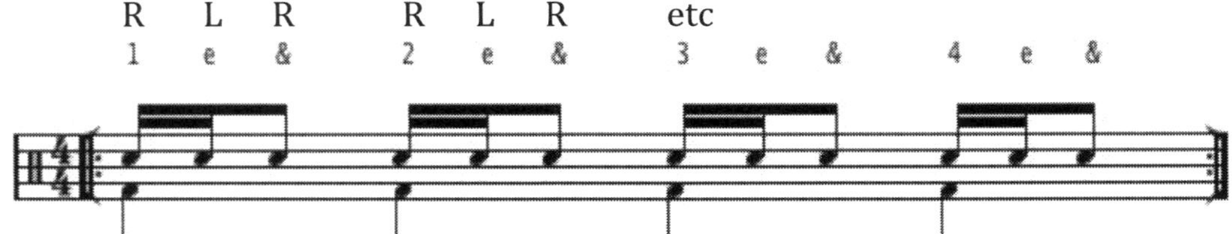

This next bar is played exactly the same as the bar above. Imagine two 1/16s and an 1/8.
Ex.2

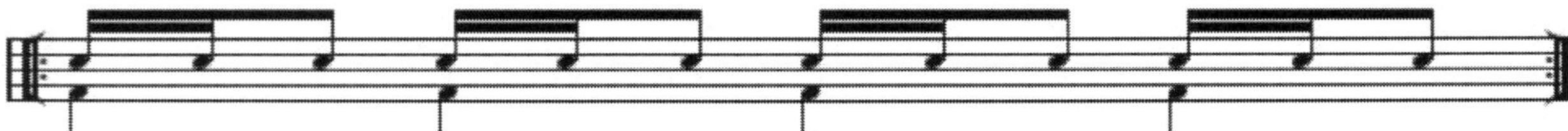

Ex.3

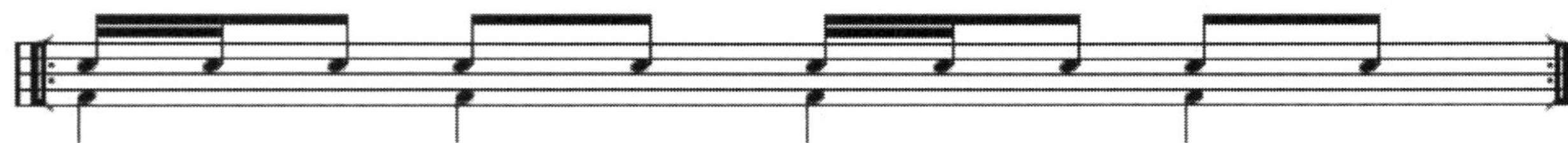

Ex.4

Play these bars as fills with one bar of a high hat rhythm. Try with the rhythms on the last page.

Video 10

More groups of 16th notes

These additions to standard groups of 16s will start to build very interesting rhythms and fills.

Ex.1 Notice the gap in the group of 1/16s here. Imagine the second note is left out.
Note the sticking.
Count...

This next bar is played exactly the same as the bar above.
Ex.2
See 1/8 and two 1/16s here.

The rhythm in Ex.4 is called a rumba. It is a Latin American dance beat.

Here's a four bar rumba piece to try out. Note the variation in bar three and try your own.

Add the crash cymbal with the right hand on the first beat.

Rhythms and fills

Play each two bar example and repeat until smooth and fluent. Then play three bars of the rhythm and make the fill be the fourth bar.

Ex.1

Take each line by itself and using the rhythm of each fill bar change the drums you choose in different orders to see how many variations you can come up with on that same rhythm.

Practise tips:

- Regular practise is the very best way to make progress on the drums.
- Try to do some practise every day. Set up a regular time to practise and divide the time you have into three sections.
- *First section:* Work on rudiments like the singles, doubles and paradiddles at the beginning of this book. Experiment with them and come up with your own ideas.
- *Second section:* Work on the exercises and pieces in the book that you find challenging and keep working at them. You will eventually get them sounding good.
- *Third section:* Just play! No books. Make up your own rhythms, discover new ideas, and work on making the grooves you play really solid and sounding good. Have fun !!

Play Away

Play this piece slow and steady at first. Then try and build the speed up to 120 bpm.
High hat (Second time through play on ride cymbal and add hi hat with foot if you can).

Video 11

Two hands playing together

Practise with right hand on the hi hat and then with the ride cymbal.

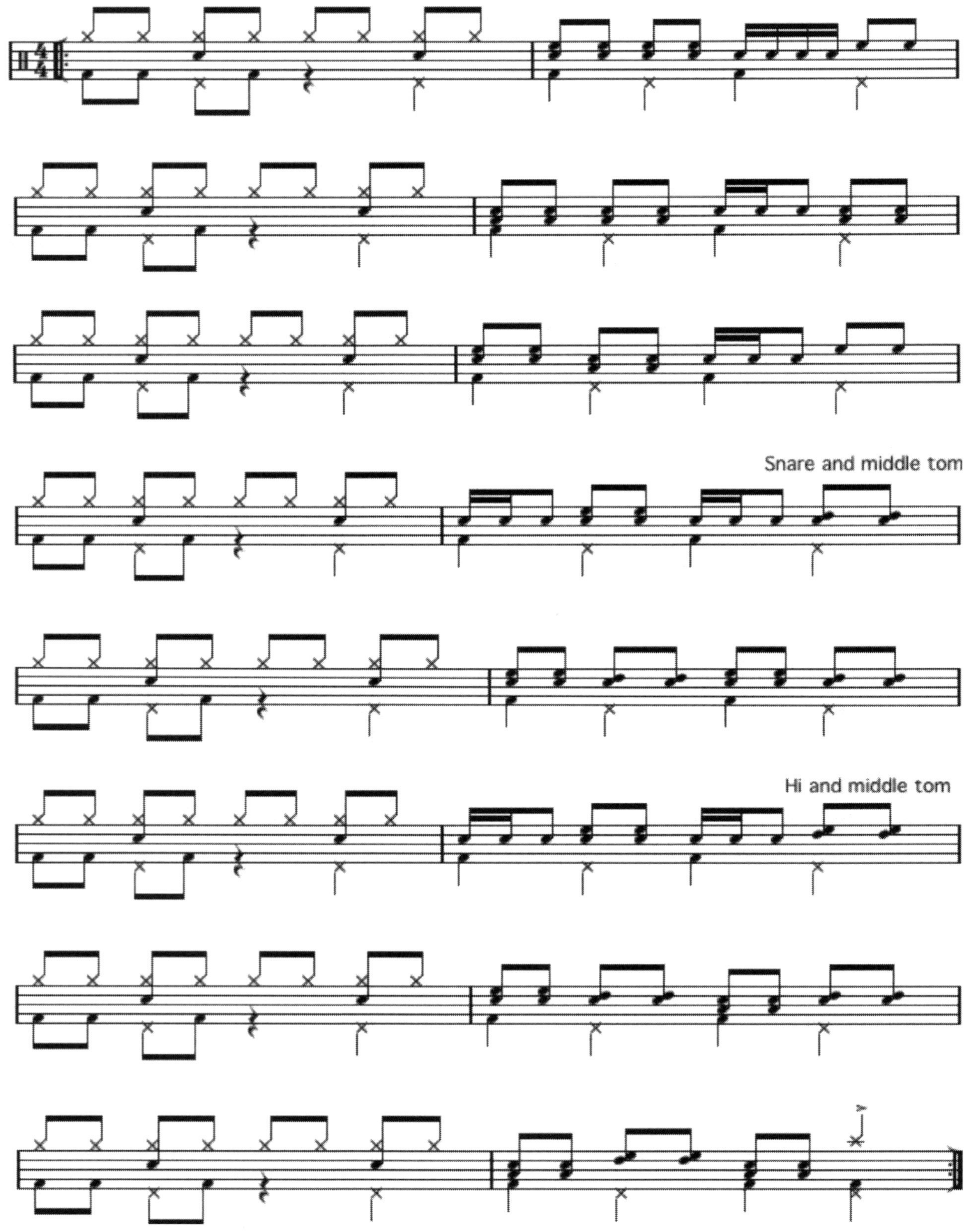

First beat on the toms & open hi hats

Play these 16s with the very first beat on the toms.

Below is a basic samba rhythm. Also try with feet alternating bass drum and hi hat.

The three bars below have the high hat being opened with the foot on the notes marked with an 0. Lift your toes off the hi hat pedal and close down on the next 1/8 note beat.

Add this idea to all the examples you have worked on in the book so far.

Video 12

A basic Latin beat

The bell of the ride cymbal is the small circular raised bit in the middle. When it's hit with the shaft of the stick (6-7cms down from the tip) it gives a strong clear tone which is a big part of the 'Latin sound' on the drum kit.

Bell of cymbal

Play quarter notes on the bell, with any fill you like on the fourth bar.

Bell of cymbal

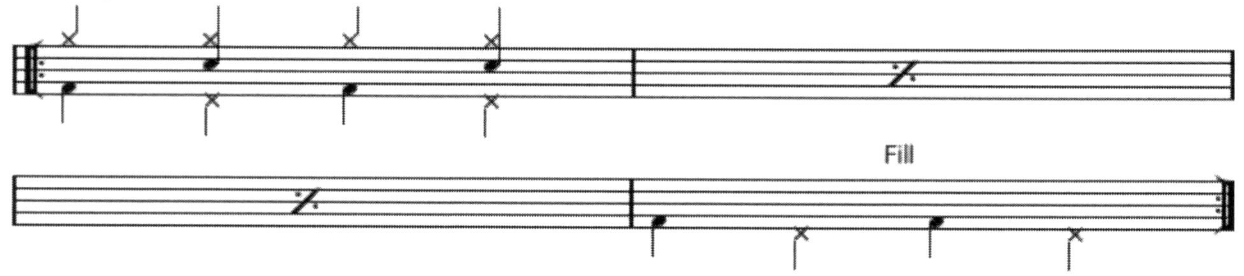

Fill

Now move the left hand, on the fourth beat to the high tom.

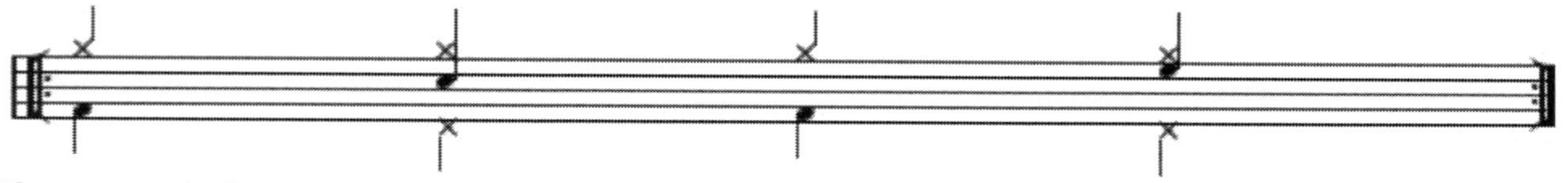

Play two 1/8th notes with the left hand, on the fourth beat on the high tom.

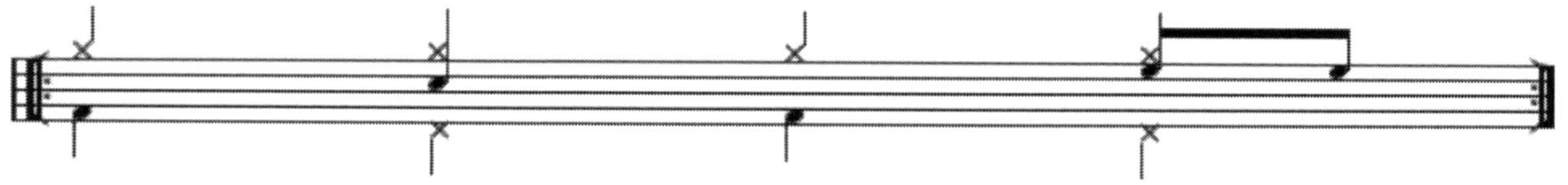

Last add two 1/8th notes on the bell, with the right hand on the third beat.

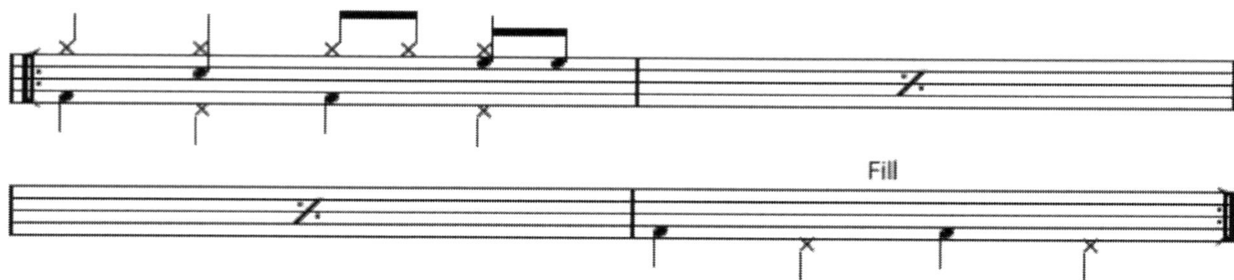

If you are keen, go back to page 21 and play that page with quarter notes on the bell.

Video 13

3:4 Time signature

We have learned that the time signature tells us how many, and what kind of beats we have in each bar. 4:4 is four quarters notes in each bar. On this page we are looking at 3:4 time signature, that is three quarter notes in each bar.

Ex.1

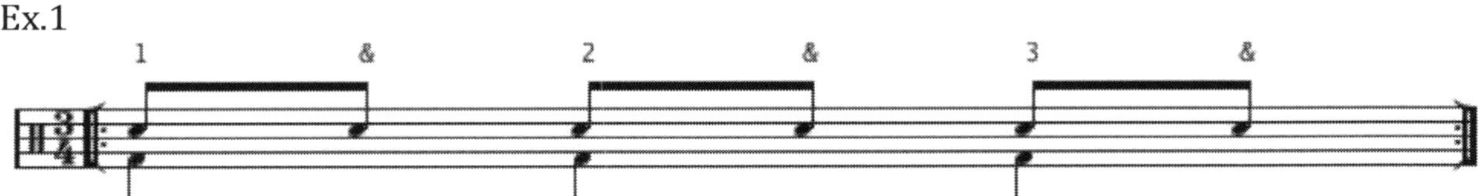

Now with 16s on first beat.

Ex.2

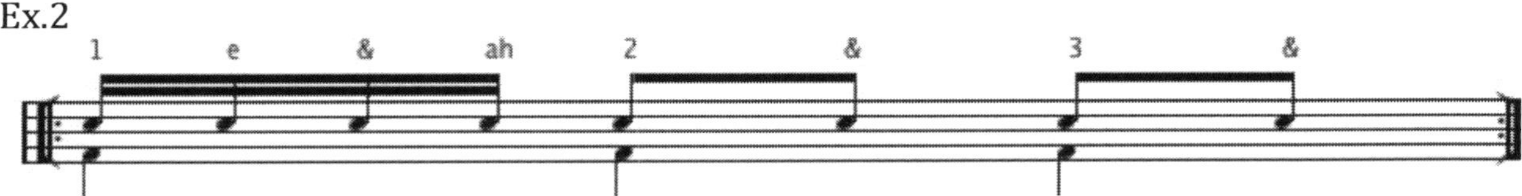

As Ex.2 played around the kit. Practise around any toms you like.

Ex.3

Now introduce the hi hat, with left foot on beats two and three.

Ex.4

Ex.5

8s rhythm in 3:4. Right hand on ride cymbal.

Ex.6

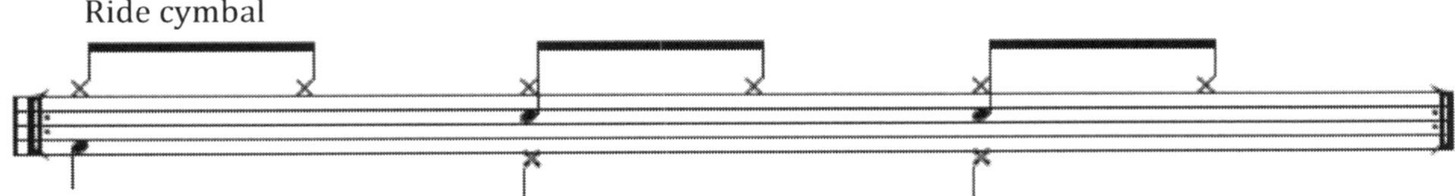

Rhythm and fill together. Now three bars of rhythm, and then one bar fill. Experiment!

Ex.7

Snare variations

Until now we have mostly used the snare on beats two and four. We can also play it on any of the other 1/8 note beats within the bar.
Make up grooves and add your own fills to the ideas below.

The snare can also play 'fours'. That's playing on every quarter note.

Ex.5 Ex.6

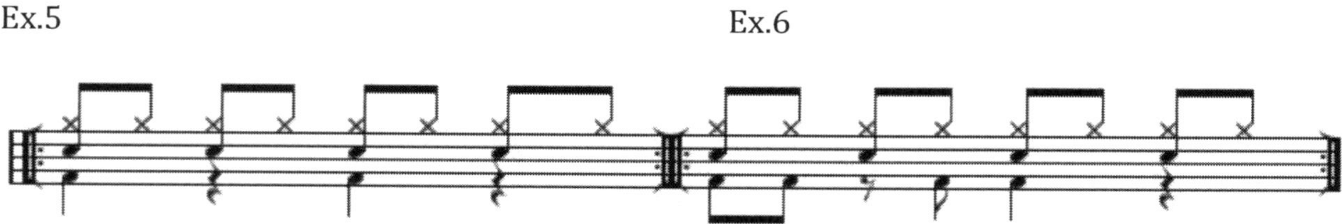

Also place the snare 'off' the beat. That's the & beats. Discover your own ideas.

Short fills and tom tom rhythms

Fills can be for a whole bar or longer as we have seen previously, or even just for one beat as in Ex.1, or two beats in Ex.2, and three beats in Exs. 3 & 4.

Here's a rhythm with 8s played on the toms instead of the hi hat or cymbal. The left hand still plays two and four on the snare.

Anything goes in drumming! Discover your own ideas.

Play the above four bars then alternate with four bars on the hi hat.

Combining Styles

Notice in this piece how playing different styles together can work to good effect.
Also note the dynamics (changing from quiet to loud etc.)

Video 14

1/8th note triplets

Triplets are three beats playing the space of two. They are joined by one beam at the top and have a figure 3 over them. Be aware that as they are an odd number of beats (3) for each quarter note, the hands will alternate right to left with each quarter note played with the feet. See Ex.1.
This time signature can also be shown as 12:8, that's twelve 1/8 notes in each bar

Ex.1 Count

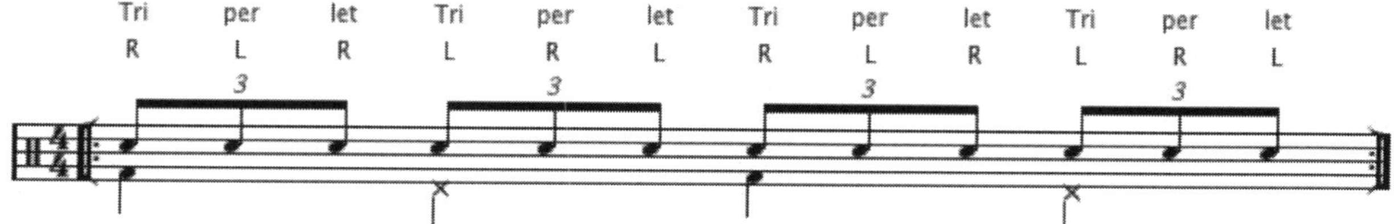

Ex.2 Around the kit.

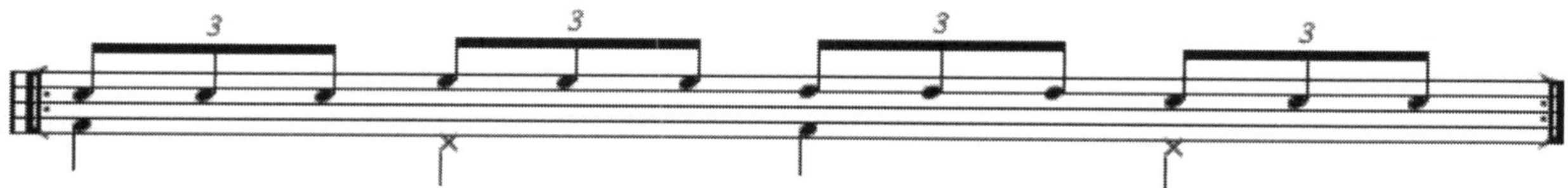

Ex.3 With the first beat of each triplet on the toms. Mind the sticking!

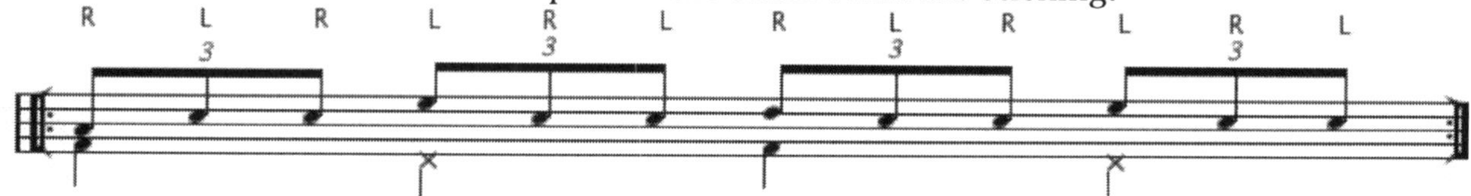

Ex.4 (Ride Cymbal) Here's a rhythm with triplets on the ride cymbal.

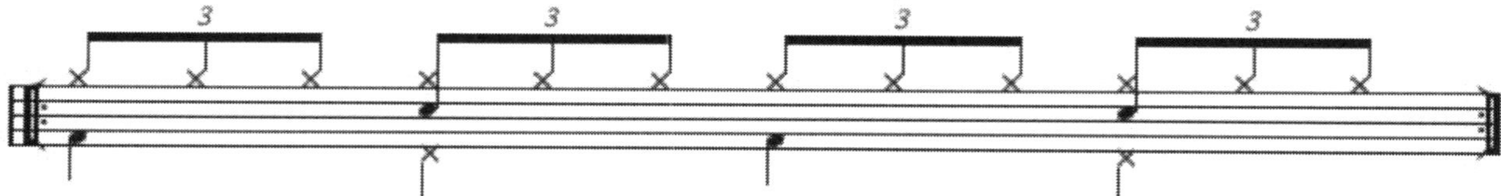

Ex.5 (Ride Cymbal) One bar of rhythm and one bar fill.

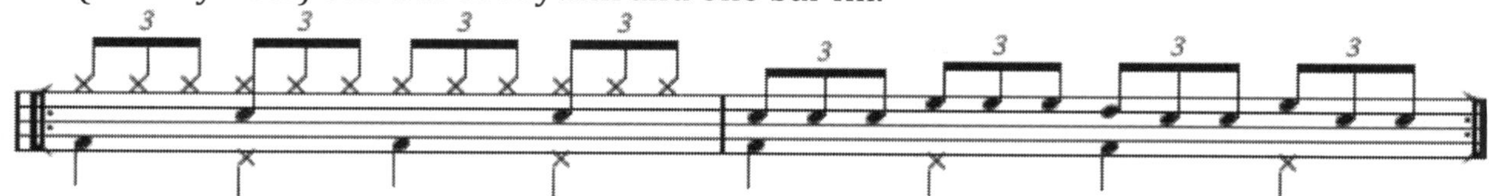

Ex.6 (Ride Cymbal) Add an extra bass drum on the third triplet note of the second beat.

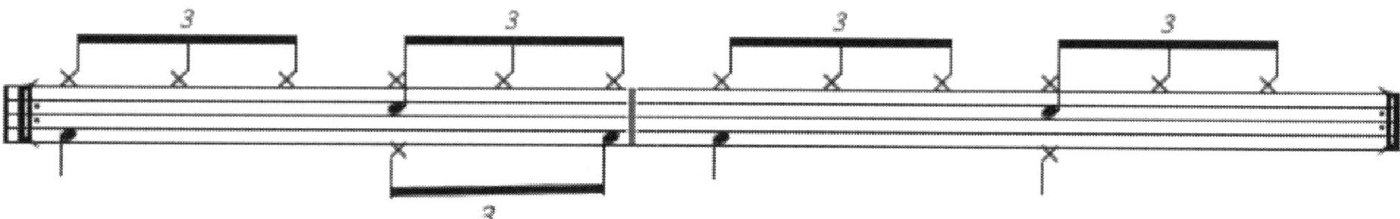

The shuffle

The Shuffle is based on triplets except we leave out the middle beat of each group. It has a swing feel, or like a trotting horse type of feel to it. It is able to achieve faster speeds than the (12:8) triplet beat.
Still count the triplets out, or count 1 &2 &3 &4 etc. with a triplet swing to it.
(Exercises. 1 & 2 are with the right hand on the high hat)
Ex.1 Say or count LOUD

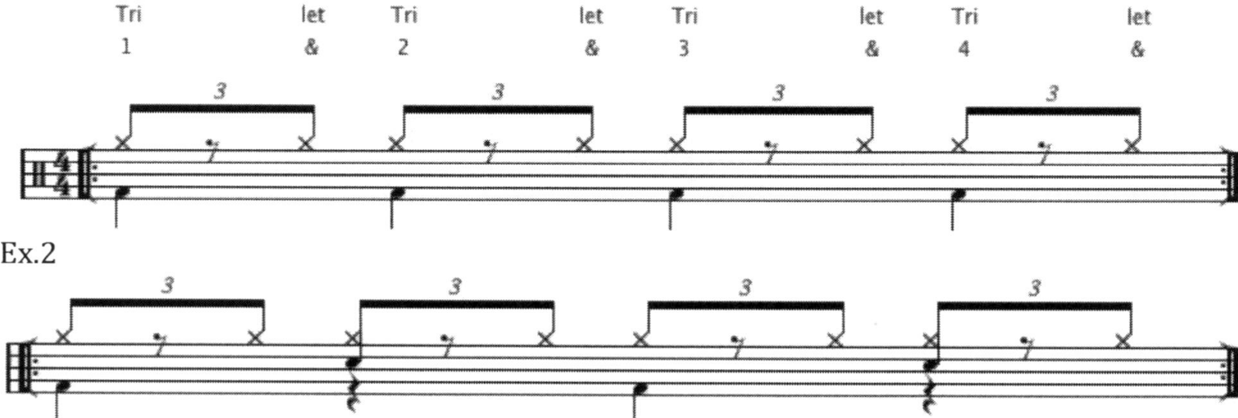

Ex.2

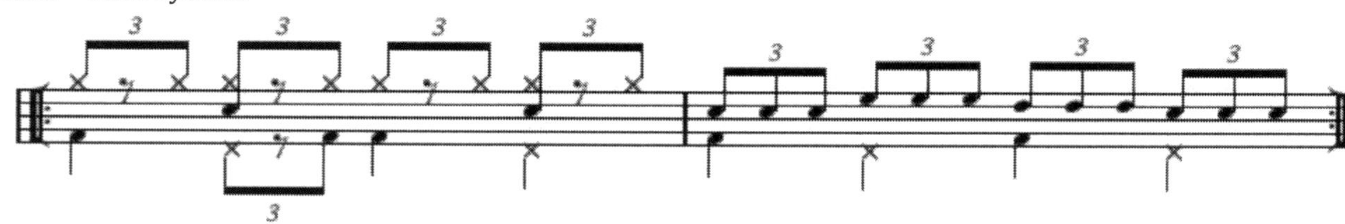

With bass drum addition and triplet fill.
Ex.3 Ride Cymbal

Playing quarter notes with a swing feel.
Ex.4 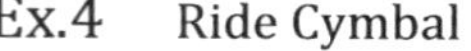

With a jazz swing, ride cymbal rhythm.
Ex.5 Ride Cymbal

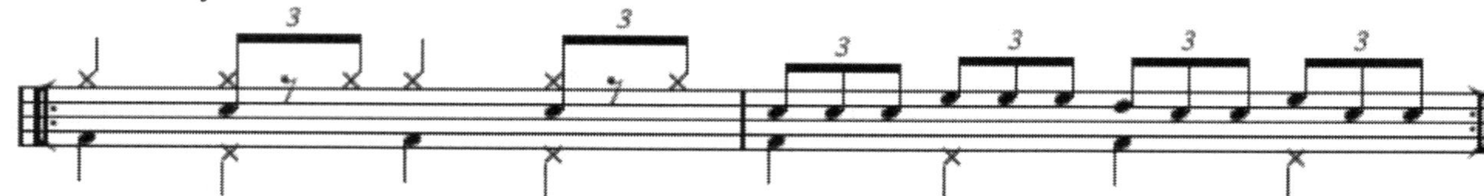

Playing the snare on just the third beat gives Ex.6 a half time feel.
Ex.6

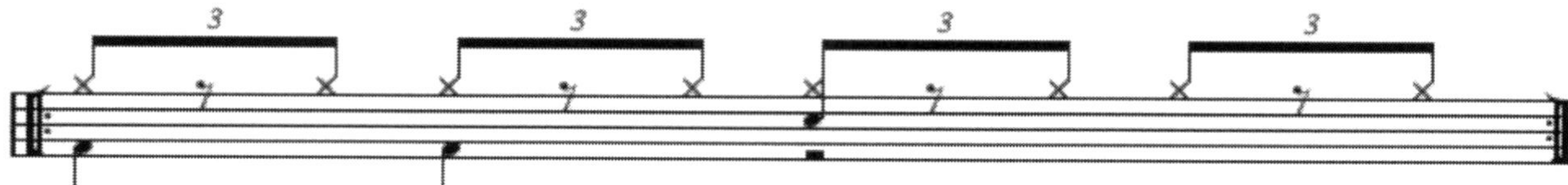

Video 15

Funky 16s on the hi hat

16s on the high hat are typically associated with 'Funk' music. Keep the high hats tightly closed, and go for a controlled smooth and even 16s rhythm. Playing with the tips of the sticks in the middle of the top high hat cymbal produces the desired sound.

Ex.1 High hat

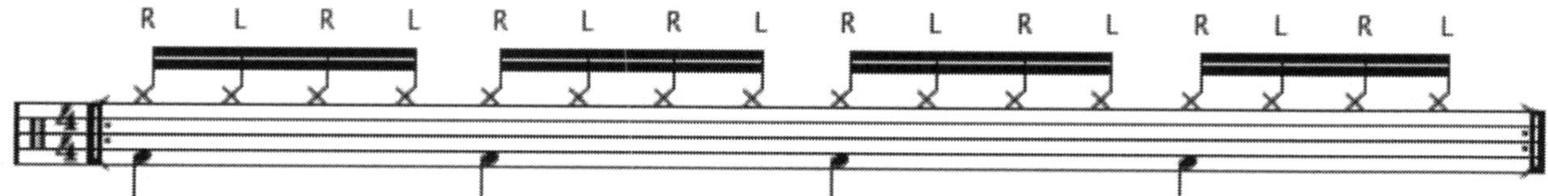

Bring the right hand onto the snare on beats two and four.

Ex.2

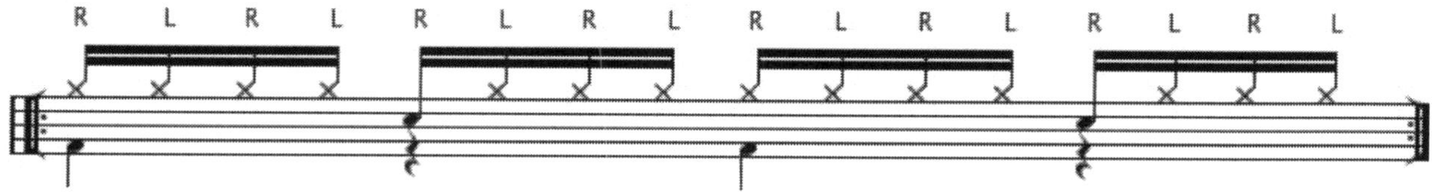

Try this bass drum variation, and all the others on page 21, with 16s on the high hat.

Ex.3

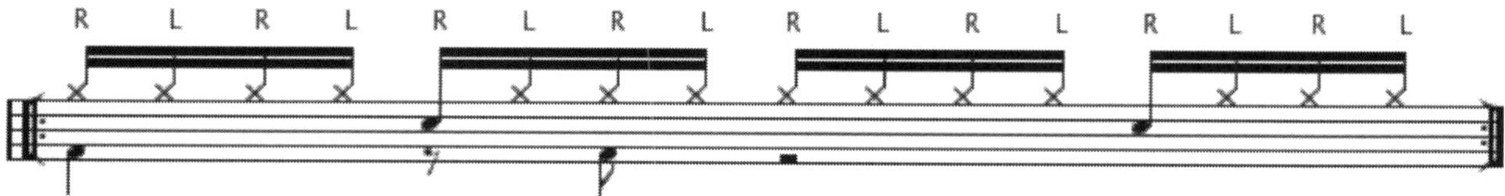

Notice the snare on the fourth 1/16 of the second beat. Count 1 e & ah 2 e & ah etc.

Ex.4

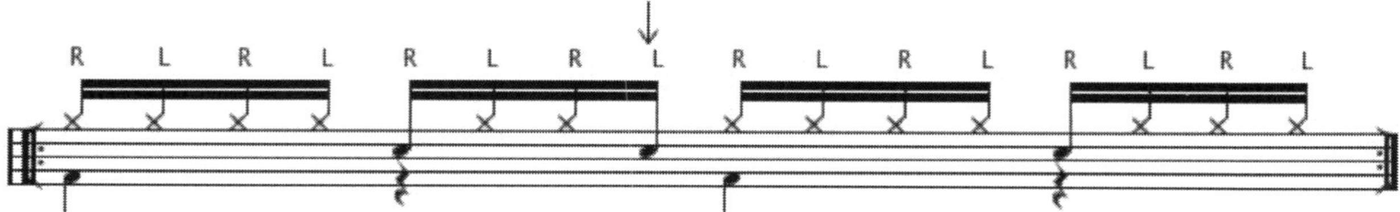

Notice the left hand snare on the second 1/16 of the first beat.

Ex.5

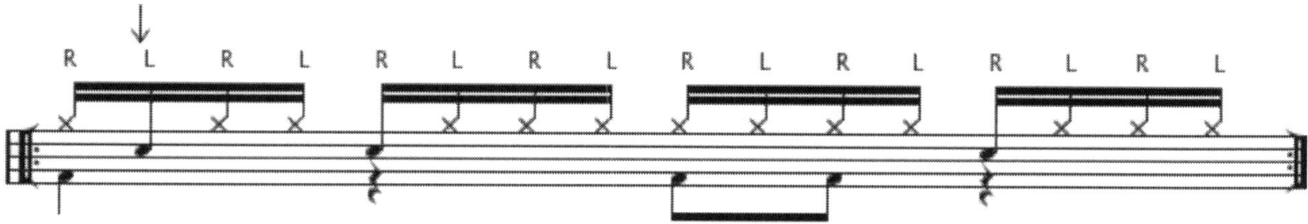

In Ex.6 the notes marked differently on the snare are left hand 'ghost' notes. Play them gently while you play the second and fourth beats loud with the right hand accent.

Ex.6

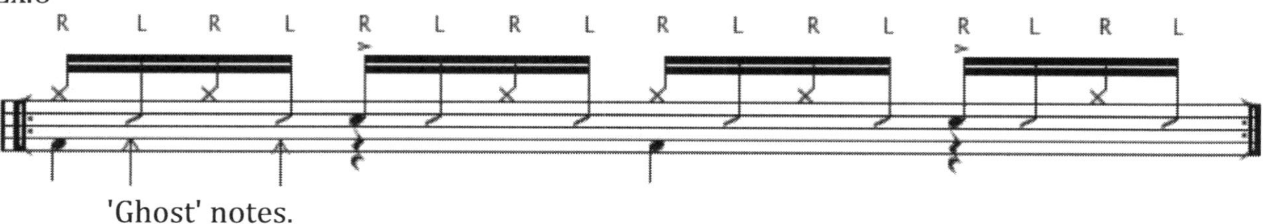

'Ghost' notes.

Video 16

Show Time

Show Time... continued

Congratulations on completing this book. Well done!
Now for the next step up -
'The Easy Way to Advance Your Drumming' Book/CD,
Available from www.stevelaffy.co.uk

Printed in Great Britain
by Amazon

37243735R00020